Do You KNOW Your BRIDE?

by Dan Carlinsky

sourcebooks

Published by Sourcebooks, Inc.
P.O. Box 4410, Naperville, Illinois 60567-4410
(630) 961-3900
Fax: (630) 961-2168
www.sourcebooks.com

Library of Congress Cataloging-in-Publication Data
Dan Carlinsky
Do you know your bride? / by Dan Carlinsky.
    p. cm.

Printed and bound in China.
OGP 22

You may think you know almost everything there is to know about the woman you've chosen to be your bride. Trust us, this little book will show that really, you don't.

No matter how long you two have known each other, no matter how much you've talked—about matters both serious and foolish—there's plenty you haven't yet learned about her.

This hundred-question quiz will help you to educate yourself, so grab a pencil and see how you do. You won't find the answers in the book, of course. For those, you'll have to check with your woman. When you do, you'll find yourselves talking *to* each other *about* each other: your likes and dislikes, your beliefs and opinions, and stories and facts about your pasts.

They're little things, sure, but they aren't insignificant. They're the bits and pieces that make up who we are. And knowing about them is much more than collecting mere personal trivia. Knowing is caring.

Score ten points for each correct answer (taking partial credit wherever you can) and rate yourself according to this scale:

Above 900: What a performance!

800-900: Very good for a couple just starting out.

600-790: Pretty good. You'll improve as time goes by.

Below 600: Ask your bride for a remedial course.

Good luck.

— D.C.

1. NAME AT LEAST ONE FOOD YOUR BRIDE WOULD NEVER WANT TO GIVE UP.

_____

2. HAS YOUR BRIDE EVER PLAYED POOL OR BILLIARDS?

_____ Yes, and she's pretty good at it.

_____ Yes, but she's not all that sharp.

_____ No, never.

3. HAS SHE EVER PLUNGED A TOILET?

_____ Yes

_____ No

4. OR JUMPED ON A TRAMPOLINE?

_____ Yes

_____ No

5. IS THERE ANY RELATIVE OR FRIEND SHE'S CURRENTLY NOT SPEAKING TO?

_____ Yes: _____

_____ No

6. WHAT COLOR M&M'S DOES SHE FAVOR?

_____

7. WHAT COUNTRY, IF ANY, DOES YOUR BRIDE MOST WANT TO VISIT?

_____

8. HAS SHE EVER GOTTEN SEASICK?

_____ Yes, once

_____ Yes, more than once

_____ No

9. IN A BOOKSTORE, WHICH SECTION DOES SHE HEAD FOR FIRST?

_____

10. TRY TO NAME FOUR THINGS YOUR BRIDE NEVER LEAVES HOME WITHOUT.

_____

_____

_____

_____

11. HOW DID SHE VOTE IN THE LAST BIG ELECTION? (OR DID SHE SIT IT OUT?)

_____

12. IF YOU'RE BUYING YOUR BRIDE A GIFT OF CLOTHING, WHAT COLOR SHOULD YOU NEVER, EVER CHOOSE?

_____

13. OF ALL HER FRIENDS AND RELATIVES, WHO HAS A HOUSE OR APARTMENT SHE'D MOVE TO IN A MINUTE?

_____

14. HOW DOES SHE SIGN HER NAME ON A FORMAL DOCUMENT? HOW DOES SHE PLAN TO SIGN AFTER SHE'S MARRIED?

Now: _____

After marriage: _____

15. IF SOMEONE OFFERED YOU A FREE WEEKEND ON A PRIVATE ISLAND—JUST YOU TWO IN THE WHOLE PLACE—SHE'D SAY:

_____ "Great! When do we go?"

_____ "Uh...you mean we'd be all alone at sea? With no one around? What if...?"

16. WHICH FRIENDS, NEIGHBORS, OR RELATIVES, IN HER OPINION, HAVE RAISED SPOILED BRATS?

_____

17. WHICH OLDER COUPLE DOES YOUR BRIDE LOOK TO AS A ROLE MODEL FOR YOUR MARRIAGE?

_____

18. IF SERVED A WHOLE STEAMED OR BOILED LOBSTER, WOULD SHE:

_____ Know how to eat it like a real pro?

_____ Know enough to slog her way through it?

_____ Not know where to start?

19. WHO TAUGHT HER TO DRIVE A CAR?

_____

20. DOES SHE EVER EAT SOMETHING STRAIGHT FROM THE FREEZER THAT SHOULD BE DEFROSTED?

_____ Often

_____ She's done it

_____ Never

21. HAS SHE EVER THROWN SOMETHING AWAY AND THEN REGRETTED IT?

_____ Yes: _____

_____ Never

22. IS THERE ANYONE SHE HASN'T BEEN IN TOUCH WITH FOR A LONG TIME BUT SHE'D LOVE TO HEAR FROM?

_____ Yes: _____

_____ No one

23. ICE CREAM IN A CONE OR A CUP?

_____ Cone

_____ Cup

24. HAS SHE EVER GOTTEN AN AUTOGRAPH OR A SIGNED PHOTO OF A CELEBRITY? DOES SHE STILL OWN IT AND KNOW EXACTLY WHERE IT IS?

_____ Yes: _____, and it's in _____.

_____ No

25. DID SHE KEEP A DIARY OR JOURNAL AS A GIRL?

_____ Yes, for a few weeks or months

_____ Yes, for the better part of a year

_____ Yes, for a year or more

_____ She never kept one

26. IS HER FAVORITE CLOTHES SHOPPING IN:

_____ Bargain stores?

_____ Department stores?

_____ Small, personal shops?

_____ Thrift shops or charity shops?

27. WHEN NERVOUS, DOES SHE:

_____ Munch nonstop?

_____ Not eat a thing?

_____ Talk a blue streak?

_____ Shut up like a clam?

_____ Fidget, tap, and squirm?

28. IF SOMEONE AT WORK OFFERS TO TELL HER A RAUNCHY JOKE, YOUR BRIDE REPLIES:

_____ "Let's hear it."

_____ "I'd rather you didn't."

_____ "Don't bother—I know 'em all."

29. RUSHING TO AN IMPORTANT DAYLONG MEETING, SHE NOTICES A TEAR IN HER SLEEVE. WILL SHE:

_____ Go home and change, even though she'll be late?

_____ Get there on time and try to hide the tear all day?

_____ Get there on time and ignore the problem?

_____ Get there on time and explain what happened with a laugh?

30. WILL YOUR BRIDE ADMIT TO BEING ANY OF THESE?

_____ Impulsive	_____ Workaholic
_____ Stubborn	_____ Spoiled
_____ Easily annoyed	_____ A closet eater
_____ Shy	_____ Gullible
_____ A tease	_____ A neat freak

31. WITH PEOPLE SHE KNOWS CASUALLY, IS SHE BETTER AT REMEMBERING:

_____ Faces?

_____ Names?

_____ Both?

_____ Neither?

32. HAS SHE EVER CALLED A RADIO TALK SHOW AND APPEARED ON-AIR? WOULD SHE?

_____ She has and she'd do it again.

_____ She has but once is enough.

_____ She hasn't but would.

_____ She hasn't and wouldn't dream of it.

33. HOW MANY OF THE ORIGINAL THREE STOOGES CAN SHE NAME?

_____ Zero

_____ One

_____ Two

_____ Three

34. CAN SHE TIE A MAN'S NECKTIE?

_____ Yes

_____ No

35. CAN YOU NAME AT LEAST ONE SUMMER JOB OR PART-TIME JOB SHE HELD WHILE IN SCHOOL?

_____

36. DID SHE EVER HAVE A CRUSH ON A TEACHER? (TEN BONUS POINTS IF YOU KNOW WHO.)

_____ Yes: _____

_____ No

38. SHOULD OTHER PEOPLE'S KIDS CALL HER BY HER FIRST NAME?

_____ Sure, she prefers it.

_____ She'd rather they didn't.

_____ Either way is fine with her.

37. IF SHE HAS PLENTY OF TIME, DOES SHE PREFER:

_____ A bath?

_____ A shower?

39. WHEN WAS THE LAST TIME SHE WENT TO A MOVIE ALONE?

_____ Within the past month

_____ Within the past year

_____ More than a year ago

_____ Probably never

40. WOULD SHE TAKE THE LAST COOKIE ON THE PLATE?

_____ Why not?

_____ Yes, but she'd feel guilty about it.

_____ She just couldn't.

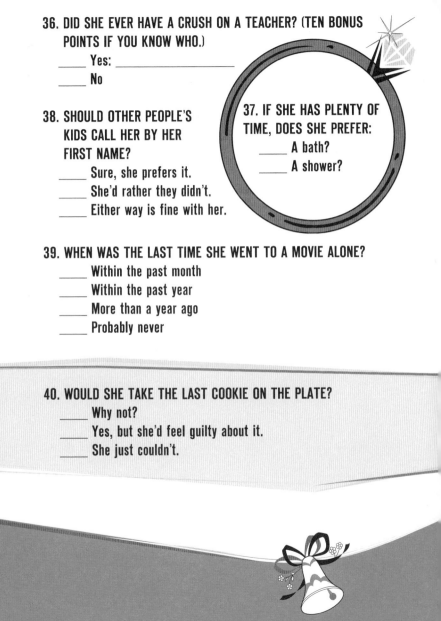

41. "MONEY MATTERS SHOULD NEVER BE DISCUSSED IN FRONT OF THE KIDS." SHE WOULD:
_____ Agree
_____ Disagree

42. "WHAT DID THE SNAIL SAY AS HE RODE ON THE TURTLE'S BACK?" "WHEEEE!" YOUR BRIDE WILL RATE THIS JOKE:
_____ Hysterically funny
_____ Silly but worth a chuckle
_____ Simply stupid

43. WHICH OF THESE SCARE HER?
_____ Thunder and lightning
_____ Snakes
_____ Heights
_____ Stinging insects

44. DOES SHE HAVE ANY PHOTOS OR PAINTINGS OF HER GRANDPARENTS OR EARLIER ANCESTORS?
_____ Yes, pictures of _____
_____ No

45. DOES SHE REMEMBER MORE OR LESS THAN YOU DO ABOUT THE FIRST TIME YOU MET?

_____ More

_____ Less

_____ About the same

46. NAME TWO TEACHERS SHE HAD IN GRADE SCHOOL.

_____

_____

47. DOES SHE KNOW HER BLOOD TYPE? (DO YOU?)

_____ Yes: type _____

_____ No

48. HER TYPICAL DAY ALMOST ALWAYS INCLUDES:

_____ Doing a crossword

_____ Doing another kind of puzzle

_____ Checking her horoscope

_____ Exercising

_____ Weighing herself

_____ Phoning her best friend

49. DOES SHE KNOW HOW TO PLAY:

_____ Bridge?

_____ Blackjack?

_____ Poker?

_____ Go fish?

50. IF YOU WERE OFFERED A GREAT JOB FOR TWO YEARS A THOUSAND MILES AWAY, WOULD SHE GO:

_____ Willingly?

_____ Reluctantly?

_____ Kicking and screaming?

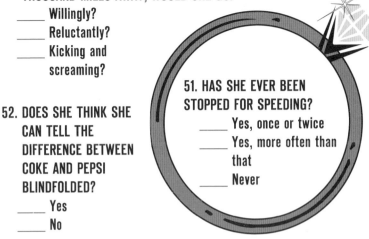

51. HAS SHE EVER BEEN STOPPED FOR SPEEDING?

_____ Yes, once or twice

_____ Yes, more often than that

_____ Never

52. DOES SHE THINK SHE CAN TELL THE DIFFERENCE BETWEEN COKE AND PEPSI BLINDFOLDED?

_____ Yes

_____ No

53. DOES SHE KNOW:

_____ What an Allen wrench looks like?

_____ What spackle is used for?

_____ How to describe a Phillips screw?

54. SHE'S MOST LIKELY TO CONTRIBUTE VOLUNTEER TIME TO WHICH KIND OF CHARITY?

_____ Religious

_____ Environmental

_____ Child-related

_____ Elderly-related

55. HAS SHE EVER DYED HER HAIR AN UNUSUAL COLOR OR PAINTED HER NAILS A STRANGE SHADE?

_____ Hair
_____ Nails

56. YOU'RE HIKING WITH FRIENDS IN AN UNFAMILIAR PLACE AND COME TO A SIGN: "PRIVATE PROPERTY." ONE FRIEND SAYS, "THEY'RE TRYING TO STOP HUNTERS AND CAMPERS, NOT US." YOUR BRIDE SAYS:

_____ "That's right. Let's go ahead."
_____ "'Private Property' means private property. We shouldn't trespass."
_____ (turning to you) "What do _you_ think?"

57. AS FAR AS SHE'S CONCERNED, WHEN A BABY CRIES IN A RESTAURANT:

_____ The parents should remove the child quickly.
_____ Others in the room should lighten up and live with it.

58. HOW DOES SHE LIKE SLEEVELESS T-SHIRTS ON MEN?

_____ They're hot.
_____ On the right guy, they're hot.
_____ They're OK.
_____ She detests the look.

59. CAN SHE TOUCH HER ELBOWS TOGETHER BEHIND HER BACK?

_____ Yes

_____ No

60. HAS SHE EVER ADDED A QUART OF OIL TO A CAR ENGINE?

_____ Yes

_____ No

61. DOES SHE THINK DRESSING TWINS ALIKE:

_____ Is cute?

_____ Is OK sometimes?

_____ Can do psychological damage to the kids?

62. WOULD SHE LIKE FREE LESSONS IN:

_____ Ballroom dancing?

_____ Cabinet making?

_____ Pastry baking and decorating?

_____ Calligraphy?

63. HAS SHE EVER BEEN AN OFFICER OF A CLUB OR ORGANIZATION?

_____ Yes: _____

_____ No

64. SHE THINKS HANGING AROUND ALL DAY IN PJ'S OR A NIGHTSHIRT, NOT ONCE GOING OUT, IS:

_____ Decadent but a wonderful way to spend a day now and then.

_____ Perfectly fine any time.

_____ Something only losers do.

65. WHAT'S THE LONGEST SHE'S EVER TALKED ON THE PHONE IN ONE SESSION?

_____ Less than an hour

_____ One to two hours

_____ Two to four hours

_____ Longer than four hours

66. WHICH CHOICES WOULD SHE MAKE?

_____ Dog	or	_____ Cat
_____ Pencil	or	_____ Pen
_____ Rock	or	_____ Rap
_____ Chocolate	or	_____ Vanilla
_____ Sunday in church	or	_____ Sunday at the beach

67. WHEN SHE SHOPS FOR CLOTHES, DOES SHE LOOK FIRST TO A PARTICULAR:

_____ Store?	_____ Style?
_____ Brand?	_____ Color?

68. SHE THINKS OLD-FASHIONED NAMES FOR KIDS ARE:

_____ Cute

_____ Solid and traditional

_____ Stuffy

69. WHICH OF HER FRIENDS, MALE OR FEMALE, HAS A NAME SHE REALLY LIKES?

_____

70. IS THERE A FOREIGN LANGUAGE SHE'D LOVE TO LEARN?

_____ Yes: _____

_____ No, she's satisfied with what she knows

71. HAS SHE EVER LAUGHED SO HARD THAT SHE PEED HER PANTS?

_____ Once or twice

_____ More than that

_____ So far, never

72. WHAT'S HER IDEA OF COMFORT FOOD?

_____

73. HAS SHE EVER LOST A RING?

_____ Yes

_____ No

74. DOES SHE LOOK AT NEWSPAPER COMIC STRIPS? WHICH ONES?

_____ Yes: _____

_____ No

75. DOES SHE THINK ANY OF THESE SHOULD BE LEGALIZED EVERYWHERE?

_____ Marijuana

_____ Gambling

_____ Prostitution

76. WHICH DESCRIPTIONS APPLY TO HER RELATIONS WITH HER PARENTS?

_____ Her mother and she are pretty good friends.

_____ Her mother disapproves of much of what she does.

_____ She's embarrassed to be seen with her mother.

_____ She and her father have a nice relationship.

_____ She doesn't talk to her father all that much.

_____ She's always in conflict with her father about something.

77. IF YOUR BRIDE COULD HAVE HER CHOICE OF PLASTIC SURGERY PROCEDURES MIRACULOUSLY DONE WITH NO PAIN, NO SCAR, AND NO RECOVERY PERIOD, AND AT NO COST, WHAT WORK WOULD SHE CHOOSE? OR WOULD SHE WANT NOTHING DONE AT ALL?

_____

78. DOES SHE OFTEN READ MORE THAN ONE BOOK OR MAGAZINE AT A TIME?

_____ Yes, she goes back and forth as the mood strikes.

_____ No, she sticks with one until she's finished it.

79. HAS SHE EVER BEEN:

_____ Really drunk?

_____ Lost in a parking lot?

_____ So happy or touched that she cried?

_____ Unable to stop laughing in a quiet public place?

80. WOULD HER IDEAL NEW YEAR'S EVE BE SPENT:

_____ At home, just the two of you?

_____ With a small group of friends or relatives?

_____ At a big party?

_____ In a giant outdoor crowd?

81. WHEN SHE'S HOME ALONE, DOES SHE GENERALLY:

_____ Turn on the radio for background?

_____ Turn on the TV?

_____ Play recorded music?

_____ Enjoy the quiet?

82. HOW DOES YOUR BRIDE RANK THESE QUALITIES IN A MAN?

_____ Sex appeal _____ Sense of humor

_____ Smarts _____ Reliability

_____ Charm and politeness

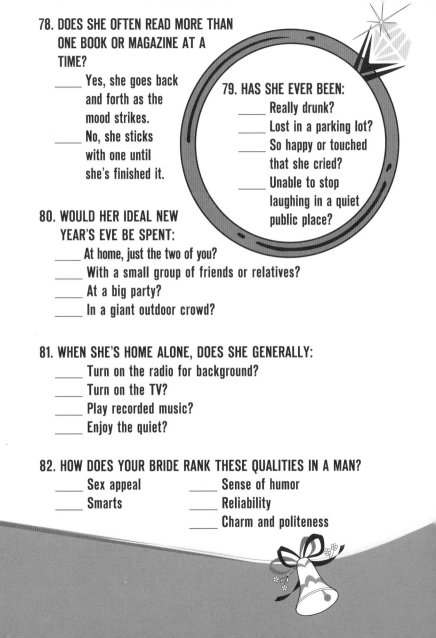

83. WHICH OF HER MARRIED FEMALE FRIENDS AND RELATIVES DOES SHE THINK FOUND THE ALL-AROUND BEST HUSBAND?

_____

84. SHE THINKS GUYS WITH THINNING HAIR:
_____ Should do something about it…quick.
_____ Shouldn't worry.
_____ Can be really sexy.

85. IF SHE WERE LOOKING TO BUY A DOG, WOULD SHE PREFER ONE:
_____ From a breeder, to be sure of what she's getting?
_____ From a pound, to save a dog from being gassed?
_____ From anywhere, as long as the dog is cute?

86. DOES SHE THINK USING FOUL LANGUAGE AROUND A TODDLER:
_____ Is unwise, since kids pick up their behavior from adults?
_____ Is no big deal, since the kid's going to learn the words sometime?
_____ Can lead to some funny incidents, so the more the merrier?

87. DOES SHE FAVOR THE DEATH PENALTY:
_____ For every murder conviction?
_____ In certain rare circumstances?
_____ In no case at all?

88. WHICH STATEMENTS HIT HOME WITH HER?

_____ If CDs or books aren't in some kind of logical order, I go nuts.

_____ I cut all the food on my plate into bite-sized pieces before starting to eat.

_____ If the phone rings after ten o'clock at night, I jump.

_____ I can wrap a gift better than any store can.

_____ If a drawer or cupboard door is open, I close it.

89. "A WOMAN CAN NEVER HAVE A MAN AS A BEST FRIEND BUT NOT A LOVER." DOES YOUR BRIDE:

_____ Agree?

_____ Disagree?

90. DOGS AND CATS ON THE FURNITURE? SHE THINKS:

_____ If you want nice things, pets have to be taught to stay on the floor.

_____ Pets are more important than chairs and sofas, so let 'em up.

_____ It depends on the animal.

91. THE LAST TIME SHE BOUNCED A CHECK?

_____ During the past month

_____ During the past year

_____ Can't remember—it was ages ago

_____ Never

92. HOW MANY RINGS DOES YOUR BRIDE ORDINARILY WEAR, ANYWHERE ON HER BODY?

_____ None
_____ One
_____ Two
_____ Three or more

93. CAN SHE WHISTLE:

_____ Any tune you name?
_____ Just a few faint tweets?
_____ A loud, fingers-in-the-mouth screech?
_____ Not a peep?

94. WHEN DID SHE LAST THINK SERIOUSLY ABOUT A DRASTIC HAIRSTYLE CHANGE?

_____ Within the past month
_____ Within the past year
_____ More than a year ago
_____ Never

95. WHEN SHOPPING FOR THESE STAPLES, IS SHE LOYAL TO A SINGLE BRAND OR DOES SHE SHOP BY PRICE OR AVAILABILITY?

Loyal	Not	
_____	_____	Shampoo
_____	_____	Mayonnaise
_____	_____	Beer or cola
_____	_____	Coffee or tea
_____	_____	Laundry detergent

96. EXCLUDING FAMILY, WHO'S THE PERSON YOUR BRIDE HAS COUNTED AS A FRIEND THE LONGEST?

_____

97. IN WHICH LANGUAGES CAN SHE COUNT TO FIVE?

_____

98. DOES SHE KNOW ANYONE WITH PIERCINGS THAT ARE HIDDEN BY ORDINARY CLOTHING?

_____ Yes: _____

_____ No one

99. SHE PRAYS:

_____ Once a week, in church

_____ Once a week, on her own

_____ At least once a day

_____ Whenever she feels moved to

_____ Whenever she's very worried or stressed

_____ Never

100. CAN SHE NAME YOUR AUNTS AND UNCLES, AND THEIR CHILDREN AND GRANDCHILDREN?

_____ Every one without a miss

_____ Most of them

_____ No—when it comes to my family, she still has some learning to do

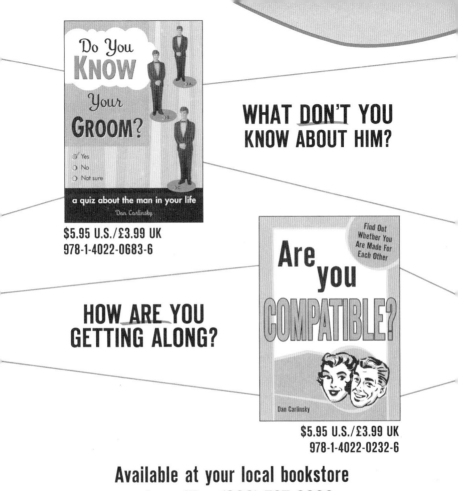